MACMILLAN READERS
INTERMEDIATE LEVEL

SIR ARTHUR CONAN DOYLE

The Sign of Four

Retold by Anne Collins

Macmillan Readers is a series of engaging narrative texts designed to stimulate learners while enhancing their language skills, building literacy and boosting reading confidence. Through captivating stories and fascinating cultural themes, learners will explore a diversity of scenarios that foster vocabulary expansion, comprehension skills and a lifelong love of reading.

The right reader at every stage
Tailored to each learner's stage of language proficiency, our six levels feature text adapted to match the skill level. With controlled vocabulary and grammar, learners can read freely and immerse themselves in the story. When more challenging words are introduced, either the text will provide sufficient context to aid understanding or a full explanation will be provided in the Glossary.

Readers for all, anywhere, anytime
Macmillan Readers are perfect for shared, guided and independent reading. Whether in traditional print, immersive audio or the convenient eBook, Macmillan Readers are equally effective for in-class activities, paired discussions or solo reading at home or on the move.

Reading for pleasure, knowledge and well-being
Regular reading and reading for pleasure:
- increases reading confidence, benefiting all literacy skills, not just reading.
- reinforces and enriches vocabulary, providing a variety of contexts.
- expands general knowledge.
- supports concentration, inner reflection and well-being.

Macmillan Readers will inspire a love for reading in English while nurturing essential language skills. Unlock new worlds, expand horizons and embark on an adventure in English!

(NOTE: While the content of Macmillan Readers is evaluated for age suitability, we kindly remind parents and teachers that they are ultimately responsible for determining whether a particular book is appropriate for their child or student.)

Contents

1	A Visitor for Sherlock Holmes	4
2	Miss Morstan's Story	6
3	A Strange Meeting	10
4	The Death of Major Sholto	14
5	The Great Agra Treasure	19
6	A Terrible Murder	22
7	The Tiny Footprints	25
8	Inspector Jones Makes an Arrest	28
9	The Dog That Loved Creosote	31
10	The Hunt Begins	36
11	Mystery on the River	40
12	Inspector Jones Receives a Telegram	42
13	The Chase on the River	46
14	The Treasure is Lost	49
15	The Sign of Four	52
	Points for Understanding	56
	Glossary	60
	Exercises	63

1
A Visitor for Sherlock Holmes

For many years, I shared an apartment in London with my friend, Sherlock Holmes.

My name is Doctor Watson. I worked as a doctor in the British Army for several years. While I was in the army, I travelled to many strange and interesting places. I had many exciting adventures.

Then one day, in Afghanistan, I was shot in the shoulder. My wound was deep and took many months to heal. I nearly died from pain and fever. At last I got better, but I could not work in the army any more. I retired from the army and came back to England.

That is why I was living in London with Sherlock Holmes. I had known my friend for many years. Our address was 221B Baker Street, in the centre of the city.

I enjoyed sharing an apartment with Holmes. My friend was a very clever man. He was the most famous private detective[1] in London. He helped to solve crimes and catch criminals.

When people were in trouble or needed help, they came to Holmes. Sometimes the police came to Holmes and asked for help in catching a criminal.

Sherlock Holmes did not care if his clients[2] were rich or poor. He enjoyed solving their interesting problems. He was very happy when he was working. It was the most important thing in his life.

One afternoon, I was reading a book and Holmes was standing by the window in our sitting room. Usually he was very busy and active. But this afternoon he did not seem very happy. I was worried about my friend.

'What's the matter with you today, Holmes?' I asked.

A Visitor for Sherlock Holmes

'Come and stand at the window, Watson,' Holmes said. Look out into the street. See how uninteresting London is today.'

It was winter. The street outside was almost empty. Everyone was at home in front of their warm fires.

'I need some work, Watson,' said Holmes impatiently[3]. 'I cannot live without interesting problems and mysteries. That's why I became a private detective. I love my work. It keeps my brain active. But when there are no crimes and no mysteries to solve – ah, then life becomes very boring for me.'

He turned sadly away from the window.

At that moment, there was a knock at the door. Our housekeeper[4] came into the room. She was carrying a small white card on a silver tray[5]. Holmes picked up the card.

'Miss Mary Morstan,' he read aloud. 'I don't know anyone of that name. Please ask the lady to come in. Perhaps it is a new client.'

A few moments later, Miss Morstan entered the room. She was young and not very tall, with blonde hair and blue eyes. Her clothes were not fashionable, but they were clean and tidy. She had a lovely face. I noticed at once that she looked worried and unhappy.

'Please sit down, Miss Morstan,' said Holmes kindly. 'I am Sherlock Holmes and this is my good friend, Doctor Watson. Doctor Watson and I have worked together many times.'

'I'm very pleased to meet you both,' said the young lady. Then she turned to Holmes and looked at him with her lovely blue eyes.

'Mr Holmes, I've heard that you give people good advice. I'm not a rich woman but I hope you can help me too. Something very strange has happened. Mr Holmes, I need your help!'

2

Miss Morstan's Story

Holmes rubbed his hands together excitedly. His eyes shone and he leant forward in his chair.

'Tell us your story,' he said.

Miss Morstan began her story and we listened.

'My father,' she began, 'was a captain in the army. When I was very young, he was sent to India. My mother was dead and I had no other relatives in England. So, while my father was away, I was sent to school.

'When I was seventeen, I received a letter from my father. He said that he was leaving India and coming back to England. He

Miss Morstan's Story

gave me the address of a hotel in London. He asked me to meet him there.

'I was very happy and excited about seeing my dear father again. I went to London and arrived at the hotel. I asked for Captain Morstan, my father. But I was told by the hotel manager that my father was not there. He had gone out the night before and not returned.

'I waited all day and all night, but my father didn't come back to the hotel. Finally, I went to the police. They advertised[6] for Captain Morstan in all the newspapers, but without success. I never saw my dear father again.'

Miss Morstan began to cry.

Holmes opened his notebook. 'What was the date that your father disappeared?' he asked.

'It was 3rd December 1878 – nearly ten years ago.'

'What happened to his luggage?'

'It was still at the hotel,' replied Miss Morstan. 'The cases contained some books and clothes, and some paintings and ornaments[7] from the Andaman Islands.'

'The Andaman Islands. What are they?' I asked.

'A small group of islands near the coast of India,' said Miss Morstan. 'There is a prison on one of the islands. My father was one of the officers in charge of the prisoners. He worked there for many years.'

'Did your father have any friends in London?' asked Holmes.

'Only one – Major Sholto. He was also in charge of the prisoners in the Andaman Islands. The Major had retired from the army some time before my father disappeared. He was living in London and, of course, I went to see him. But he didn't know that my father had arrived in England.'

'Your story is very interesting,' said Holmes, rubbing his hands together once more. 'Please, go on.'

'Four years after my father disappeared,' continued Miss Morstan, 'I saw an advertisement in the newspaper. The date

Miss Morstan's Story

was 4th May 1882. To my surprise, the advertisement asked for the address of Miss Mary Morstan. It said that if I advertised my address, I would receive some very good news.'

'What did you do?' asked Holmes.

'I advertised my address in the same newspaper. The next day, I received a small cardboard box. Inside the box was a lovely pearl. And I have received another five pearls since that day. They arrive every year on the same day. Look.'

She opened a flat box and showed us six beautiful pearls.

'There was no letter with the pearls?' asked Holmes.

'Nothing at all,' replied Miss Morstan. Then she continued. 'But the strangest thing of all happened this morning. That is why I came to see you. This morning, I received a letter. Please read it.'

Miss Morstan's Story

'Thank you,' said Holmes. He took the letter and studied it carefully. Then he handed it to me.

London
17th November 1887

Dear Miss Morstan,
   Go to the Lyceum Theatre tonight at seven o'clock. Stand outside the entrance, on the left. If you are afraid, bring two friends. Do not bring the police.
   You have been deceived, but you will learn the truth tonight.
                                                    Your Unknown Friend

---

'What can this letter mean?' asked Miss Morstan. 'I am afraid. What should I do, Mr Holmes? You are a clever man and can give me good advice.'

Holmes jumped up excitedly.

'We shall go tonight to the Lyceum Theatre – the three of us, you and me and Doctor Watson. The letter asks you to bring two friends with you. You will come with us, won't you, Watson?'

'Of course,' I said. 'I'll be very happy to come.'

I was speaking the truth. I wanted to help Miss Morstan.

'You are both very kind,' said Miss Morstan. 'Since my father disappeared, I have been alone in the world. I have no friends whom I can ask for help. What time shall we meet this evening?'

Holmes looked at his watch.

'It's now half past three,' he said. 'Come back at six o'clock. Don't be afraid, Miss Morstan. This evening we'll come with you to the Lyceum Theatre. We'll meet your unknown friend. And we'll try to solve the mystery.'

'Thank you,' said Miss Morstan. She smiled at us and left the room.

'What a lovely woman,' I remarked.

'I'm going out now,' said Holmes. 'I'll be back in about an hour.'

A Strange Meeting

When Holmes had gone I sat down by the window and tried to read a book. But I could not stop thinking about Miss Morstan. I hoped that we would be able to help her.

3
==

A Strange Meeting
================

At half past five, Holmes returned. He was very pleased about something.

'I have had great success, Watson,' he said, as I gave him a cup of tea.

'What, Holmes ! Have you solved the mystery already?' I asked in surprise.

'No, no. But I have discovered something very interesting. Miss Morstan said that her father had a very good friend in India. His name was Major Sholto.'

'Yes,' I said. 'Major Sholto had retired from the army. He was living in London when Captain Morstan disappeared. But he did not know that Morstan was in England.'

'Well,' said Holmes. 'I have just been to the offices of *The Times* newspaper. I looked through the old copies of the newspaper[8] and I discovered that Major Sholto died on 28th April 1882.

'Perhaps I am very stupid, Holmes, but I don't see why this discovery is interesting.'

'Listen,' Holmes said. 'Captain Morstan disappeared. He had one friend in London – Major Sholto. But Major Sholto said that he didn't know that Captain Morstan was in London.

'Four years later, on 28th April 1882, Sholto died. A few

A Strange Meeting

days later, on 4th May 1882, Captain Morstan's daughter saw the advertisement in a newspaper. Then, she received a valuable present. These presents came every year. Why do the presents arrive on that day? They must have something to do with Sholto's death.'

I was still puzzled. 'But Sholto died six years ago,' I said. 'Why did Miss Morstan receive that letter today – six years later? The letter speaks of telling her the truth. What can it mean?'

'I hope that we'll find the answers to these questions tonight, Watson,' said Holmes seriously. 'Are you ready? It's six o'clock and here is Miss Morstan.'

Miss Morstan entered the room. She was wearing a dark cloak and hat. She did not seem afraid, but her beautiful face was very pale.

I picked up my hat and my heaviest stick. I noticed that Holmes took his gun from his drawer and put it into his pocket.

We got into a cab[9] and were soon on our way to the Lyceum Theatre. In the cab, Miss Morstan took a piece of paper out of her bag.

'Mr Holmes, I forgot to show you this. This note was found in my father's luggage. It is very strange. I don't know what it means. Perhaps it isn't very important, but I wanted you to see it.'

Holmes unfolded the note carefully and spread it on his knee. He took a magnifying glass[10] out of his pocket and examined the paper.

'This paper was made in India,' he remarked. 'Have a look at it, Watson.'

I took the note and studied it carefully. The paper was thin and old. There was a drawing on the paper.

'It looks like the plan of a large building,' I said. 'Somebody has made a mark to show a certain place in the building. But what are

A Strange Meeting

these names at the bottom? And what is the meaning of – "The Sign of Four"?'

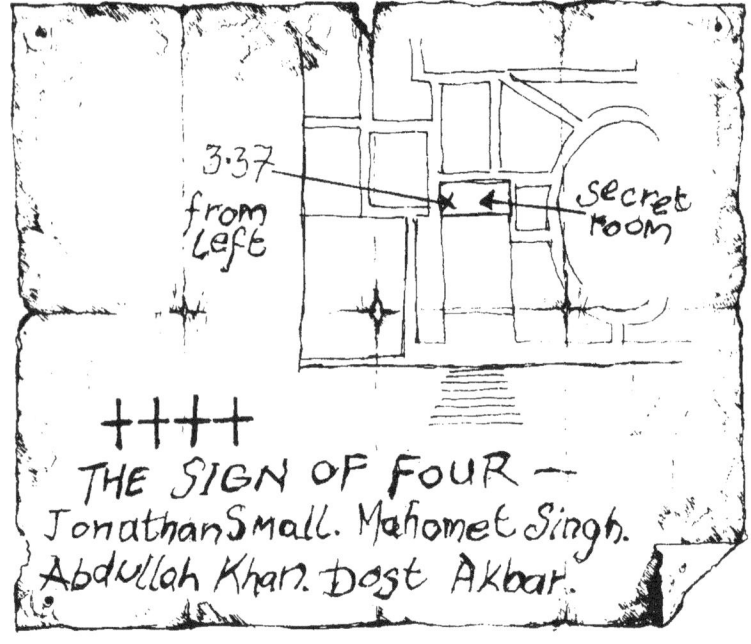

'I don't understand what this note means,' said Holmes. 'But it might be important. I will keep it.'

He sat back in the cab. Miss Morstan and I talked quietly together. But Holmes did not say anything. I knew he was thinking hard.

It was getting dark and the people in the streets were hurrying home from work. I was feeling a little afraid. I wondered what kind of person we would meet at the Lyceum Theatre.

There were many people outside the theatre. Everyone was meeting friends and going in to see the play. The letter had told us to stand outside on the left. We waited. Suddenly a small dark man appeared.

A Strange Meeting

'Are you Miss Morstan and her friends?' he asked.

'Yes,' she said.

'You must promise me that these men are not policemen,' said the stranger.

'They are not policemen,' replied Miss Morstan.

'Then come with me,' said the man.

He led us quickly across the street to another cab and opened the door. We went inside. The man closed the door and jumped up onto the driver's seat of the cab. The horse moved off quickly.

We passed through so many streets that I was very soon lost. I had no idea where we were going. I was feeling nervous and Miss Morstan's face looked white. Sherlock Holmes was calm. Our strange driver did not turn round or speak to us. The only sound was the noise of the horse's hooves.

At last we stopped. We were outside a house in a dark quiet

street. It had only one small light in the kitchen window. There were no lights in any of the other houses in the street.

We knocked at the door. It was opened immediately by an Indian servant. The Indian was wearing a bright yellow turban on his head. He had white clothes and a yellow belt. It was very strange to see such brightly coloured clothes in this quiet street in London.

'My master is waiting for you,' said the servant.

As he spoke, we heard a man's voice. It came from one of the rooms inside the house.

'Bring them in to me,' the voice called. 'Bring them straight in to me.'

4
The Death of Major Sholto

We followed the Indian servant into the house. He stopped in front of an open door.

'Come in, come in,' said the voice.

We entered – Holmes, Miss Morstan and myself – and were astonished[11]. The room in which we were standing was full of Indian paintings and ornaments. The carpet was soft and very thick. There were two large tiger skins on the walls.

In the centre of the room stood a strange little man with a bald head. He was smiling, but he seemed very nervous.

'My name,' said the bald-headed man, 'is Thaddeus Sholto. You are Miss Morstan, of course. And these two gentlemen . . .?'

'This is Mr Sherlock Holmes and this is Doctor Watson.'

'A doctor!' cried Thaddeus Sholto excitedly. 'Oh, please could you listen to my heart? I am very worried about my heart.'

I listened to his heart beating. But I could hear nothing wrong

'My name,' said the bald-headed man, 'is Thaddeus Sholto.'

The Death of Major Sholto

with it. 'There is nothing wrong with your heart,' I told him.

'I'm so glad,' said Thaddeus Sholto. 'Miss Morstan, your father had a very weak heart. If his heart had been stronger, he would have been alive today.'

Miss Morstan sat down and her face turned very white.

'I knew that he was dead,' she said. There were tears in her eyes.

I was very angry with Thaddeus Sholto. He did not notice how much he had upset Miss Morstan.

'Please tell us why we have been brought here,' said Miss Morstan. So Thaddeus Sholto began his strange story and we listened.

'My father,' Sholto said, 'was Major Sholto of the Indian Army. He retired from the army about eleven years ago. He bought a house in North London. He called the house Pondicherry Lodge. My brother, Bartholomew, and I were his only children. We knew that Captain Morstan - Miss Morstan's father - and our father had been very good friends in India. When we heard that Captain Morstan had disappeared, we were very upset. My brother, Bartholomew, and I also knew that our father was afraid of something. He never went out alone. He often spoke about a man with a wooden leg who followed him. He seemed very afraid of this man.'

'Did he tell you why he was afraid?' asked Holmes.

'No, he didn't,' Thaddeus Sholto replied. Then he continued with his story.

'One day in 1882, our father received a letter from India. This letter upset him very much. He became ill. Every day he grew weaker. At last, he was dying. He asked to see me and my brother, Bartholomew. We went to his room. He told us to lock the door and come over to the bed. Then he held our hands and spoke to us. He said that he wanted to tell us the truth about

The Death of Major Sholto

Captain Morstan's death. He was the only person who knew this terrible secret.

'When Father was in India with Captain Morstan, they found a great treasure. It was called the Great Agra Treasure. The jewels in this treasure were worth more than a million pounds. Father brought the Agra Treasure back to England. Morstan followed him and came at once to the house to ask for his share[12]. But the treasure had made Father greedy. He did not want to give any of it to Morstan. He wanted to keep it all for himself. Morstan became very angry. They had a terrible argument. Father knew that Morstan's heart was weak. Suddenly, the colour of Morstan's face changed. Father saw at once that Morstan was dead. He did not know what to do. He had not killed Morstan. But he was afraid that people would believe that he had killed Morstan. He decided to say nothing. He hid the body and he also hid the Great Agra Treasure.

'Soon the news of Morstan's disappearance spread through London. Only our father knew the terrible truth. He told us as he was dying that he had been a wicked and greedy man. He said that he had acted very wrongly. But that he had paid for his crime. The Agra Treasure never brought him happiness – only fear and guilt[13]. Then he told us that Captain Morstan had a daughter called Mary. He asked us to listen carefully. Then he began to tell us where he had hidden the treasure. At that moment a terrible change came over our father's face. He pointed at the window and cried out in a voice full of fear, "Keep him out! Keep him out!"

'My brother and I stared at the window. We saw a horrid face looking in through the window. It was wild and had a black beard and cruel eyes. We rushed to the window but the man had gone. When we went back to the bed, Father was dead.'

'What did you do then?' asked Holmes.

The Death of Major Sholto

'We ran out into the garden,' replied Sholto. 'We looked everywhere, but we found nothing. In the morning, we went to our father's room. We found that someone had been in the room during the night. There was a piece of paper on the bed beside my father's body. And on this paper some words were written. These words were "The Sign of Four".'

5
The Great Agra Treasure

Holmes, Miss Morstan and I looked at each other in surprise. My body felt cold with fear.

'The same words – "The Sign of Four" – were written on that strange note in Captain Morstan's luggage,' said Holmes.

'What can it mean?' I whispered.

Miss Morstan turned to Thaddeus Sholto.

'Why did you send me the pearls?' she asked.

'On the table, beside our father's bed, was a gold cup,' Sholto answered. 'It was decorated with six pearls. Our father had told us that this cup was part of the Agra Treasure. He had wanted us to share the treasure with you. So we found your address and sent you the pearls, one by one.'

'That was very kind of you, Mr Sholto,' said Miss Morstan.

'Not at all,' said Sholto. 'But now I am going to tell you something very exciting. Yesterday my brother and I found the Great Agra Treasure!'

'You found the treasure!' we repeated in astonishment.

'Yes. Our father had died before he told us where it was hidden. My brother, Bartholomew, and I searched for the treasure for six years. Yesterday, we found it. That is why we sent you the letter, Miss Morstan. We have found the treasure. But half of it belongs to you.'

'Where is the treasure now?' asked Holmes.

'At my father's house, Pondicherry Lodge,' replied Sholto. 'My brother, Bartholomew, lives there now. We must go there immediately so that Miss Morstan can see the treasure and claim her share. Bartholomew is expecting us. Miss Morstan, tonight you will be a rich woman!'

Miss Morstan was going to be very rich. I should have been very

The Great Agra Treasure

happy. But I did not feel happy at all. I had fallen in love with Miss Morstan. But I did not have very much money. If she became rich, I could not ask her to marry me.

Thaddeus Sholto put on his coat. 'Come,' he said. 'I have a cab waiting outside. It will take us to Pondicherry Lodge. We must not be late.'

It was a long drive to Pondicherry Lodge. The night was cold, and the moon was shining brightly. As we sat in the cab, Thaddeus Sholto continued to talk. Holmes, Miss Morstan and I listened.

'My brother, Bartholomew, is a very clever man,' he said. 'He knew that the treasure was somewhere in the house. He had an idea. He measured the height of the house outside. It was seventy-four feet high. Then he measured the height of the rooms inside the house. He added the heights of the rooms together. The total was only seventy feet. There was extra space under the roof! My brother made a hole in the ceiling of the room on the top floor. He found a secret room. Inside this little room, the treasure chest[14] was standing. Last night, I helped Bartholomew to lower the chest down into the room below. We opened the chest with a key which we found beside it.'

Thaddeus Sholto's voice became excited.

'Inside the treasure chest were hundreds of beautiful jewels – diamonds, rubies, sapphires and many others. They shone so brightly that they hurt our eyes. Miss Morstan, the Agra Treasure is really wonderful. But here is Pondicherry Lodge. We have arrived. Soon you will see the treasure for yourself.'

It was now nearly eleven o'clock. Pondicherry Lodge was a big house with a high wall around it. Everything was black and silent. There was no light except the moonlight.

'This is very strange,' Thaddeus Sholto said nervously. 'I don't understand why there are no lights. My brother,

The Great Agra Treasure

Bartholomew, is expecting us. But the house is dark.'

We walked up to the house. Suddenly we heard a noise coming from inside that great black house. It was the sound of a woman crying.

'The only woman in the house is the housekeeper,' said Sholto. 'Something is wrong.'

We hurried to the door and knocked. A tall old woman opened it. Her face was white with fear.

'Oh, Mr Thaddeus, I'm glad you have come,' she said. 'I'm very frightened. Come into the house, Mr Thaddeus. Oh, I'm glad that you are here. Something terrible has happened to your brother!'

6
A Terrible Murder

Thaddeus Sholto began to shake with fear. His face was very white.

'What do you mean?' he asked the housekeeper. 'What is the matter with my brother?'

'He locked himself in his room. He was there all day. When I knocked on the door he would not answer me,' she said. 'I knew that something must be wrong. A short time ago, I went upstairs. I looked through the keyhole of the door of his room. I saw your brother's face, Mr Thaddeus. It looks terrible. You must go up Mr Thaddeus and see for yourself.'

The housekeeper started to cry again.

'You must all go upstairs,' said Miss Morstan. 'I'll stay here and look after this poor woman.'

We left the two women – Miss Morstan and the housekeeper – downstairs. Holmes took the lamp and led the way. Thaddeus Sholto and I followed him.

We climbed up the stairs. There was a passage at the top of the stairs. At the end of the passage was a door. Thaddeus Sholto pointed to this door.

'That's the door of my brother's room,' he whispered.

We hurried forwards. Holmes turned the handle but the door was locked. Then he bent down and looked through the keyhole. He stood up again quickly.

'My God!' he cried. 'It's the work of the Devil!'

I bent down and put my eye to the keyhole. I felt very sick and afraid. The bright moonlight was shining into the room. I could clearly see a face. This face was looking straight at me. It did not move. There was a horrible smile on the face.

'This is terrible,' I said to Holmes. 'What shall we do?'

A Terrible Murder

'We must break down the door,' he replied.

We threw ourselves at the door and it broke with a sudden crack. We were inside Bartholomew Sholto's room.

Bartholomew Sholto was dead. He was sitting in a chair by a table. His body was stiff and cold. I could see that he had been dead for many hours. The dead man's body was twisted with pain. There was a horrible smile on his face.

There was a piece of paper on the body. Holmes picked it up and read it.

'Look,' he said.

In the light of the lamp, I read with horror – "The Sign of Four".

'What does it mean?' I asked.

'It means murder,' Holmes replied. He pointed to Bartholomew Sholto's ear. 'Look.'

I looked. I saw something sticking in the dead man's skin near his ear.

'It looks like a thorn[15],' I said.

'It is a thorn,' said Holmes. 'You can take it out. But be careful. It is poisoned[16].'

I took the thorn between my finger and thumb. I pulled it away easily from the dead man's skin. I looked at it. It was hard and sharp. I saw that it had poison on it.

'So this is how Bartholomew Sholto died,' I said. 'What a terrible death. But who killed him? And why?'

We had forgotten about Thaddeus Sholto. He was still standing in the doorway. Suddenly he gave a cry.

'The treasure has gone!' he cried. 'They have stolen the treasure. Look. Do you see that hole in the ceiling? We lowered the treasure down through that hole last night. After I had helped my brother with the treasure, I left him here in this room. I was the last person to see my brother alive. I heard him lock the door as I came downstairs.'

'What time was that?' asked Holmes.

The dead man's body was twisted with pain.

'It was ten o'clock. And now my brother, Bartholomew, is dead and the Great Agra Treasure has gone!'

7
The Tiny Footprints

'Go to the police station, Mr Sholto,' said Holmes. 'Ask the police to come quickly. Doctor Watson and I will wait here.'

Thaddeus Sholto turned away. We heard him going downstairs.

'Now, Watson,' said Holmes. 'We have some work to do before the police arrive. We must find out how the murderer got into the room. The door was locked. But what about the window?'

He carried the lamp to the window and examined the window sill[17] carefully.

'Look,' he said. 'Someone has come in by the window. Here is the print of a foot on the windowsill. And here is a round mark. And look on the floor – here is another footprint and another mark. And again by the table. See, here, Watson.'

I looked at the marks. Some were footprints, but some were in the shape of small circles.

'Those are not footprints,' I said.

'No,' replied Holmes. 'They are the marks made by someone with a wooden leg.'

'Someone with a wooden leg?' I said. 'Holmes! Thaddeus Sholto told us that his father was afraid of a man with a wooden leg.'

'Yes,' said Holmes. 'But the wooden-legged man was not alone. Someone else has been here too. Look outside.' We both went to the window and looked down. 'We are very high up,' said Holmes. 'A man with a wooden leg would not be able to

The Tiny Footprints

climb here by himself. Two people came into this room. We will call them Number One and Number Two. Number Two is the wooden-legged man. But who is Number One? And how did he get in?'

I looked round the room. I thought quickly. Then suddenly I knew the answer.

In the ceiling of the room was a hole. Thaddeus Sholto had told us that his brother had made this hole. The Agra Treasure had been hidden in the secret room above. The two Sholto brothers had lowered the treasure chest through this hole the night before.

A set of steps[18] was standing beneath the hole. On the floor by the set of steps was a rope.

'Number One must have looked through the hole in the ceiling,' I said. 'He saw Bartholomew Sholto sitting on the chair below him. He killed Sholto with a poisoned thorn. Then he must have taken the rope, opened the window and thrown the end of the rope down into the garden. His friend, Number Two, the wooden-legged man, must have been waiting below. Number Two climbed up the rope with the help of Number One. The murderers then lowered the treasure chest to the ground with the rope. Number Two climbed down the rope. Number One got out of the room through the hole in the ceiling.'

'Excellent, Watson,' said Holmes. 'We shall now go up and have a look at the secret room. Perhaps we can find out more information about Number One.'

We climbed the steps and found ourselves in a small dark room without any windows. There was thick dust on the floor. It was here that the treasure had been hidden for so many years.

'Look,' said Holmes. 'There is a small door in the roof. That is how Number One got in.'

Then Holmes shone the lamp down at the floor. By the light of the lamp, I saw that the floor was covered with many footprints. They showed very clearly in the thick dust. They were the prints of bare feet.

The Tiny Footprints

But they were not the footprints of an ordinary man. They were extremely small. Suddenly, a horrible thought came into my mind.

'Holmes!' I whispered. 'A child has done this terrible thing.'

Holmes did not answer. He was still studying the tiny footprints. Finally he spoke. 'No,' he said slowly. 'I don't think it was a child. Look at this footprint. Look at the marks of the toes. They are very wide apart. It is not a child's footprint. It is a man's. They are the prints of a tiny man.'

'Do you mean a dwarf[19]?' I asked in surprise.

'I will show you,' replied Holmes. 'Let's go into the room again. Let's examine once more the poisoned thorn which killed Bartholomew Sholto.'

In the room below, I picked up the thorn. I held it carefully between my fingers. I felt afraid. It was long and sharp.

'Now then,' said Holmes. 'What do you think about this thorn? Is it an English thorn?'

'No,' I said. 'It certainly is not.'

'You see,' said Holmes, 'already we begin to know many things about murderer Number One.

'He is a very small man – in other words, a pygmy[20] – from some foreign land. He is very strong and can climb great heights easily. He is also extremely dangerous. He kills people by shooting them with poisoned thorns.'

8
Inspector Jones Makes an Arrest

I looked at Holmes in astonishment.

'How strange!' I said. 'Why are a pygmy and a wooden-legged man working together? Who are these people, Holmes? And why did they kill Bartholomew Sholto?'

'They wanted the treasure, of course,' answered Holmes. 'Last night, Bartholomew Sholto was sitting in this room with the treasure. The pygmy came in through the roof and saw him. The only way to get the treasure was to kill Sholto.'

'And what about the paper with the Sign of Four?' I asked.

'It must mean revenge[21],' Holmes answered. 'Remember that a paper from the Sign of Four was also found on the dead body of Major Sholto. I don't know why someone wants revenge on the Sholto family. But we know that someone wanted revenge. They also wanted the treasure. And they were prepared to kill the Sholtos – father and son – to get the treasure.'

Holmes took out his magnifying glass and started to examine the room again. There were some bottles and tubes in one corner of the room. Bartholomew Sholto must have been interested in

Inspector Jones Makes an Arrest

chemistry. A glass tube had broken and a dark liquid had spilt onto the floor. Holmes gave a loud cry of joy.

'Come here, Watson,' he said. 'What can you smell?'

I walked over. Suddenly I smelt something very strong and unpleasant. The smell was coming from the dark liquid on the floor. 'It smells like tar,' I said.

'It is similar to tar,' Holmes answered. 'It is creosote[22].' He was smiling and rubbing his hands together.

'Why are you so pleased?' I asked.

Holmes pointed to the floor. I saw a clearly marked small footprint. I realized that the pygmy had stepped in the creosote.

'I know a dog which loves the smell of creosote. It will follow this smell for miles and miles,' said Holmes. 'We'll catch these murderers now.'

Just then we heard footsteps and loud voices outside the room.

Inspector Jones Makes an Arrest

'It's the police,' said Holmes.

As he spoke, a fat man in a grey suit entered the room. His face was red and his eyes were small and bright. He was followed by a policeman in uniform and by Thaddeus Sholto. I had never seen the fat man before, but Holmes seemed to know him well.

'Good evening, Inspector Jones,' said Holmes politely. 'Don't you remember me?'

The fat man stopped and stared. He was not very pleased to see Holmes.

'Why, yes, of course,' he said. 'You are Mr Sherlock Holmes, the private detective. Yes, I remember you well. This is an interesting crime, Mr Holmes. A man has been murdered and jewels worth a million pounds are missing. What do you think happened?'

'Well . . .' began Holmes.

But Inspector Jones did not want to listen to my friend. He thought his own ideas were better.

'Listen, Mr Holmes, I will tell you what I think,' he said importantly. 'This man, Thaddeus Sholto, tells me that he was with his brother last night. They discovered the treasure together. He was the last person to see his brother alive. Now I think that Thaddeus Sholto killed his brother. Then he ran off with the jewels.'

'Oh no, it isn't true!' cried Thaddeus Sholto.

'What about the poisoned thorn in the dead man's skin?' asked Holmes. 'And the paper with the Sign of Four?'

'The thorn belongs to Thaddeus Sholto,' replied Jones quickly. 'I don't think the paper is very important. Perhaps it's a trick. But wait a moment. What's that up there? I see a hole in the ceiling. I must have a look.'

Inspector Jones went quickly up the steps. We heard him moving about noisily in the room above. Then he came down again. He was hot and dusty.

'I know everything now,' he cried. 'I have found a door which leads out onto the roof. That was how Thaddeus Sholto escaped.'

'But the footprints . . .' began Holmes.

Inspector Jones was not listening. He had not noticed the tiny footprints. He turned to Thaddeus Sholto. The poor man was shaking with fear.

'Mr Sholto,' said Jones. 'I arrest[23] you for the murder of your brother.'

'I didn't do it!' Thaddeus said. 'Please, Mr Holmes, believe me!'

'Don't worry, Mr Sholto,' said Holmes. 'I know that you didn't kill your brother. I will find the murderer.'

Inspector Jones turned to Holmes angrily.

'Listen, Mr Holmes,' he said. 'This is a matter for the police. It has nothing to do with you. Goodnight, gentlemen.'

Inspector Jones and the policeman took Thaddeus Sholto away. A few minutes later the house was quiet again.

9
The Dog That Loved Creosote

'The police don't want my help, Watson,' said Holmes, as soon as the Inspector had gone. 'Inspector Jones thinks he has solved the crime and caught the murderer. But they have arrested the wrong man.'

I agreed with Holmes. I was sure that Thaddeus Sholto was not the murderer.

'We must be quick, Watson,' said Holmes. 'I want you to do two things. First, take Miss Morstan home. Second, go to this address – 3 Pinchin Lane. Ask for Mr Sherman. He has an old dog called Toby. I want you to bring Toby here. Meet me here in two hours' time.'

I took Miss Morstan home in Thaddeus Sholto's cab. She was

The Dog That Loved Creosote

very upset by what had happened and spoke very little. I promised that I would visit her the next day. Then I went to the address which Holmes had given me.

It was the middle of the night, and the streets of London were black and silent. As the cab went along, I thought about everything that had happened.

We had discovered the truth about some things – the death of Captain Morstan, the sending of the pearls to Miss Morstan, the advertisement, the letter. All these things were clear.

Now there were other mysteries which we had to solve. Where was the Indian treasure? What was the plan found in Morstan's luggage? Who wanted Bartholomew Sholto to die? Where were the pygmy and the wooden-legged man?

What did all these things mean? And what was the mysterious Sign of Four? I hoped that Sherlock Holmes would discover the answer to these questions.

Soon I arrived in Pinchin Lane – the address where Holmes had sent me. It was a very poor street and the houses were old and dirty. I found house number three and knocked on the door.

After some time, a face looked out from a window above. It was not a friendly face.

'Who are you?' said the face angrily. 'What do you want?'

'Come down and open the door,' I said. 'I have something to ask you.'

'Go away at once,' said the face. 'If you don't, I'll let out fifty dogs upon you.'

'My friend, Mr Sherlock Holmes . . .' I began.

At these words, the window suddenly shut and a few minutes later the door opened. I saw an old man with grey hair and a beard, holding a candle in his hand.

'Come in, sir,' he said. 'I'm Mr Sherman. I'm sorry that I was rude. I didn't know that you were a friend of Sherlock Holmes.'

I went into the small dirty house and stopped in astonishment. There were cages everywhere I looked. All the cages contained

I saw an old man with grey hair and a beard, holding a candle in his hand.

The Dog That Loved Creosote

different kinds of animals. I could see their eyes shining in the candlelight.

'What does Mr Holmes want?' asked the old man.

'A dog called Toby,' I answered.

'Toby is my best dog,' said Mr Sherman. 'He loves to follow strong smells. Especially the smell of creosote. That's his favourite.'

'That's why Mr Holmes wants him,' I said.

'Wait here. I'll go and get him.'

The old man came back after a few minutes. He was pulling a dog on a lead[24]. The dog looked very strange. It had very long ears and very short legs and its eyes were large and sad.

'This is Toby,' said Mr Sherman. 'He'll go with you. He's a friendly dog.'

The dog licked my hand and wagged its tail. I put some money into Mr Sherman's hand and the old man gave me Toby's lead.

When I got back to Pondicherry Lodge, I found Sherlock Holmes standing outside the door. He was smoking his pipe.

'Excellent, Watson!' he said when he saw me. 'You have done well. Good dog, Toby! Come here! Good dog!'

Holmes took a handkerchief out of his pocket and gave it to Toby to smell. The handkerchief was covered with creosote. The dog went mad with excitement. His sad eyes shone with happiness and his tail wagged.

'See how he loves the smell,' said Holmes. 'We won't have any problems now.'

Holmes pointed at a drainpipe[25] which went down from the roof of the house.

'While you were away, Watson,' he said, 'I went up onto the roof and discovered how the pygmy climbed up and climbed down again. He used that drainpipe.'

The drainpipe ran all the way down from the roof to the garden below. There was a large barrel full of water under the end of the drainpipe.

The Dog That Loved Creosote

'He climbed down that drainpipe and onto the barrel beneath,' said Holmes. 'It was very easy to follow his trail. He left marks everywhere. He also dropped this.'

Holmes put his hand in his pocket and took out a small bag made of dried grass. I looked inside. To my horror, I saw five or six long dark thorns. They were the same as the one which killed Bartholomew Sholto.

'The murderer has lost these,' said Holmes. 'Let's hope that he doesn't have any more. Don't touch them, Watson. They are poisoned. But come. Where's Toby? We must begin.'

Holmes took Toby's lead and pulled the dog to the bottom of the water barrel. Toby smelled all round carefully. Suddenly, he began to bark excitedly. He had found his favourite smell – the smell of creosote. Then he started to pull at his lead. 'He's on the trail!' cried Holmes. 'Let's go!'

10
The Hunt Begins

Toby pulled at his lead and ran quickly through the grass. He ran so quickly that it was difficult to follow him.

The sky was beginning to get light now. Toby ran along the paths in the garden under the trees and bushes. Then he reached the garden wall and ran along beside it. Finally, he stopped at a place in the wall where the bricks were loose.

'This is the place where they got into the garden,' said Holmes. 'It is easy to climb up and down here. Look. Do you see this mark? It is the print of a man's hand.'

He pointed at a flat stone. I saw a dirty hand print on the stone.

The Hunt Begins

Holmes picked up the dog and climbed over the wall. I followed. Toby soon found the trail again.

Toby did not look to the right or the left. He ran straight ahead with his nose to the ground. He loved the smell of creosote. Nothing could stop him from following it.

As we hurried along, I thought about the wooden-legged man and the pygmy. I wondered what would happen when we found them. I knew that they were dangerous. I wished that I had brought my gun with me.

Toby was still following the trail. Now we were passing through small narrow streets. The people were just beginning to wake up. The men were going on their way to work. The women were opening the windows and cleaning their houses.

Suddenly, Toby ran down a path. This path led straight down towards the River Thames. Soon the river appeared in front of us. Toby ran faster and faster.

The path went down to the water's edge. It ended at a small wooden jetty[26]. Toby stopped. He ran backwards and forwards trying to find the smell. He looked up at us sadly with his large eyes. He did not know what to do.

'They have got into a boat here,' said Holmes.

There was a small house beside the jetty. A notice was hanging from one of the windows. On it was written in large letters:

MORDECAI SMITH: Boats and steam launch for hire[27].

There was no one on the jetty. Several small boats were near the jetty on the bank of the river. Holmes looked at these boats.

'I wonder where the steam launch is,' he said. 'I think we must ask a few questions.'

He knocked loudly at the door of the house. A large woman with a red face opened it. A child was crying somewhere inside the house. I saw that the woman was very upset about something. She had been crying.

The Hunt Begins

'Good morning,' said Holmes politely. 'Are you Mordecai Smith's wife?'

'Yes,' replied the woman. 'What do you want?'

'Could I speak to your husband, please?' asked Holmes.

'No, you can't. He isn't here. I haven't seen him since yesterday morning.'

'Oh,' said Holmes, 'I wanted to hire a boat.'

'Well, perhaps I can help you,' said Mrs Smith. 'Which boat do you want?'

'I wanted to hire the steam launch. I have heard it is a very good boat. Let me see. What's the name? The . . .'

'The *Aurora*, sir,' said Mrs Smith.

'Oh, yes, that's right. I remember now. But where is the *Aurora*?' said Holmes, looking around. 'I don't see a steam launch anywhere.'

'Oh, sir. My husband has gone in the *Aurora*,' Mrs Smith replied and burst into tears. 'I'm very worried about him. I don't trust that wooden-legged man.'

'What wooden-legged man, Mrs Smith?' asked Holmes in a surprised voice.

'I don't know who he is, sir. But my husband went with a wooden-legged man in the *Aurora* yesterday morning and hasn't come back!'

'Oh, sir. My husband has gone in the Aurora.'

11
Mystery on the River

'I'm very sorry to hear that, Mrs Smith,' said Holmes. 'Tell me, was this wooden-legged man alone?'

'I don't know, sir. I didn't see anyone else. But it was very dark – it was three o'clock in the morning. I could not be sure.'

'What does the *Aurora* look like?' asked Holmes.

'The *Aurora* is black, sir, with two red stripes down each side. It has a black funnel[28] with a white stripe. The *Aurora* is the fastest boat on the river,' answered Mrs Smith.

Holmes looked worried.

'That's very interesting,' he said. 'Try not to worry about your husband, Mrs Smith. I am going up the river myself. If I see Mr Smith, I will tell him that I have seen you. Goodbye.'

'Goodbye and thank you,' said Mordecai Smith's wife. She had stopped crying. She went inside her house and closed the door.

'Watson, we must find Mordecai Smith and the *Aurora* as soon as possible,' said Holmes. 'Mordecai Smith and the wooden-legged man are working together. Smith has taken the two murderers in his steam launch. They are all hiding somewhere on the river.'

'It will be easy to find them,' I said. 'You must tell the police at once.'

Holmes shook his head.

'No. I don't want these criminals to know that anyone is looking for them. They will try to escape again.

'I have a better idea,' Holmes went on. 'I have many agents everywhere up and down the river. These agents are clever. I pay them to bring me information. They always know what is happening on the river. I will ask my agents to look for Mordecai

Mystery on the River

Smith and the *Aurora*. But you look tired, Watson. Let's go home and have breakfast.'

It was now nearly eight o'clock in the morning. I did feel very tired. I was glad to go home to Baker Street.

When I had had a bath and changed my clothes, I came downstairs to breakfast. Holmes was drinking coffee and reading a newspaper. 'Look, Watson,' he said. 'Here is a report about the murder of Bartholomew Sholto at Pondicherry Lodge. And about the arrest of Thaddeus Sholto by Inspector Jones last night.'

I took the paper and read the report. I felt sorry for Thaddeus Sholto. Inspector Jones had made a stupid mistake by arresting him. I knew that Sholto was not guilty of the murder of his brother. I hoped that we would be able to help Thaddeus. But would we be able to find the murderers?

Suddenly there was a loud knock on the door. A few minutes later, twelve children ran into the room.

Their clothes were dirty and ragged. They had no shoes on their feet. Their hair was untidy and their faces had not been washed for a very long time. But they seemed happy and cheerful.

'Good morning, Mr Holmes,' said the children together.

'Who are these children, Holmes?' I asked in astonishment.

Holmes laughed.

'These are my agents,' he said. 'I sent a message for them to come. Look at them. They can go anywhere, see everything, hear everything. Nobody is afraid of children.'

Holmes gave each of the children some money. Then he told them what he wanted them to do.

'You must find a steam launch called the *Aurora*,' he said.

'It is on the river somewhere and belongs to Mordecai Smith. The *Aurora* is black with two red stripes down each side. It has a black funnel with a white stripe. You must find it. Now go!'

The children ran out of the room, all talking together. They went down the stairs and out into the street.

'My agents will find Mordecai Smith and the Aurora,' said Holmes. 'Now we must wait.'

12
Inspector Jones Receives a Telegram

We had not slept all night and I was very tired. I went to bed and woke late in the afternoon. I felt much better. I went downstairs. Holmes was reading a book. I saw at once that he was worried.

'Is there any news?' I asked.

Inspector Jones Receives a Telegram

'Nothing at all. I can't understand it. I am very surprised and disappointed. My agents say that they cannot find the *Aurora*.'

'Can I do anything to help?' I asked.

'Nothing.'

'Then I'll take Toby back to Pinchin Lane. Then I'll go and see Miss Morstan and tell her what has happened.'

I went to Miss Morstan's house. She looked very pleased to see me. I told her that we had not found the treasure yet. But she did not look disappointed. I was surprised about this but I was also very pleased. I said goodbye to her and drove back to Baker Street.

I went to bed, but I could not sleep. I was thinking about Miss Morstan. I wanted to ask her to marry me. All night, I heard Holmes walking up and down in his room. Next morning, he looked tired and ill.

'My agents cannot find the *Aurora*,' he said impatiently. 'They have searched the whole river. The *Aurora* has disappeared.'

We waited all that day, but there was no news.

The next day, I woke early. It was still dark. To my surprise Sherlock Holmes was standing by my bed. He was dressed and ready to go out.

'I have had an idea, Watson,' he said. 'I am going up the river myself. Perhaps I can find the launch. You must stay here. There may be some messages.' Holmes left without another word.

That day, the time passed very slowly. I picked up a book but was unable to read it. I was thinking all the time about the wooden-legged man and the pygmy. Where were they? Why could Holmes not find them? I was worried about my friend. I knew that he was a clever detective. But perhaps this time he would not be able to catch the murderers.

At three o'clock in the afternoon, I had a visitor. It was Inspector Jones, the police officer.

I was astonished. Inspector Jones had changed completely. Two days ago, he had been very rude to Holmes. He had not wanted his help. Now he was very quiet and polite.

Inspector Jones Receives a Telegram

'Good afternoon, Doctor Watson,' said Inspector Jones. 'I'm afraid that I made a bad mistake. I have had to let Thaddeus Sholto go. Sholto has proved that he was at a friend's house when his brother died.'

Inspector Jones looked so sad that I began to feel sorry for him.

'I've received a telegram from Sherlock Holmes,' the Inspector went on. 'Here it is.'

I took the telegram and read it.

INSPECTOR JONES – GO TO BAKER STREET AT ONCE. WAIT FOR ME THERE. I KNOW WHERE SHOLTO'S MURDERERS ARE HIDING. COME WITH US TONIGHT IF YOU WANT TO CATCH THEM.

HOLMES

Inspector Jones Receives a Telegram

'That's excellent!' I cried. 'Forget about Thaddeus Sholto. You'll soon have some other prisoners, Inspector Jones.'

At that moment, the door opened and Holmes came into the room. He was smiling.

'What news?' we asked together.

'I know where the *Aurora* is,' Holmes replied. 'It wasn't on the river at all. The *Aurora* has been hidden in a boatyard[29] near the river for two days. I knew the launch at once. Mordecai Smith, the owner, was there too. He was talking to someone and he was speaking very loudly. He said that he had to have the *Aurora* ready for eight o'clock tonight. His two gentlemen were leaving for America. Their ship was waiting for them out at sea and they must not be late.

'I knew immediately what they were planning to do,' went on Holmes. 'And I know what we must do. Inspector Jones, will you help me?'

'I was wrong before and you were right,' said Jones sadly. 'I didn't listen to you then. But I'll help you now.'

'Good,' said Holmes. 'We need a fast police launch – as fast as the *Aurora*. It must be ready this evening. And two or three strong policemen to come with us.'

'I'll arrange all this,' said Jones.

'Excellent,' said Holmes. 'Tonight the three of us – you and me and Doctor Watson – will be on the police launch. We will be waiting outside the boatyard at eight o'clock. We'll be ready for the *Aurora* when she comes out. We'll catch the murderers and we'll get the treasure!'

13
The Chase on the River

At seven o'clock that evening, the three of us – Inspector Jones, Holmes and I – went down to the river. Both Holmes and I had guns in our pockets.

Inspector Jones had promised to let us use the police launch. This launch was now waiting. Four strong men were on board the launch.

Soon we were moving quickly down the River Thames. The police launch was very fast. We passed all the other boats on the river without difficulty. This pleased Holmes very much.

By eight o'clock, we had arrived opposite the boatyard where the *Aurora* was hidden. It was now dark. We waited. Ten minutes passed.

Suddenly a launch came out of the boatyard. It was black with two red stripes. It was moving very quickly.

'That's the *Aurora*!' cried Holmes. 'Follow it quickly! Faster, faster! We must catch them!'

We were going so fast that the police launch started to shake. But we could not get near to the *Aurora*.

The chase became more and more exciting. We went in and out between other boats. Many times I closed my eyes. I was sure that we would hit something.

At last we got closer to the *Aurora*. Inspector Jones turned on a light and shone it on the *Aurora*.

'Stop!' he said. 'Stop. We are the police!'

In the lamplight we could see some men on board the *Aurora*. One man was sitting at the back of the launch. Beside him was a strange dark shape.

We could also see Mordecai Smith, the owner of the *Aurora*.

'Stop!' he cried. 'Stop. We are the police!'

The Chase on the River

He was working as hard as he could. He was trying to make the engine of the launch go faster.

Inspector Jones shouted again. 'Stop!'

Suddenly, the man at the back of the *Aurora* stood up. He shouted at us angrily. He was a big strong man. Then I noticed that his right leg was missing. There was a wooden stump in its place. This was the wooden-legged man!

At the sound of the man's voice, the strange dark shape beside him moved. It was a small dark man – the smallest man I have ever seen. But the pygmy's head was large. His face was hard and cruel.

As soon as Holmes saw the pygmy, he took out his gun. I did the same.

'Shoot him if he moves his hand,' said Holmes.

At that moment, the pygmy put a short piece of wood to his lips.

We fired our guns together. The pygmy fell backwards into the water with a terrible cry.

The wooden-legged man turned the *Aurora* towards the bank of the river. As soon as the *Aurora* touched the bank of the river, he jumped out. It happened so quickly that we were not able to slow down and stop the police launch. The man had landed in the soft, wet mud of the river bank. But his wooden leg had stuck in the mud. He could not move.

We managed to turn the police launch round. We went towards the wooden-legged man and threw him a rope. Then we pulled him up over the side of our launch.

Mordecai Smith was still on the *Aurora*. But he did not try to escape. We tied the *Aurora* to our launch. The chase was over.

On the deck of the *Aurora* there was a big, heavy chest. We were sure that it contained the Agra Treasure. We carried the heavy box onto the police launch.

Suddenly Holmes stopped and pointed.

'Look,' he said.

I looked where Holmes was pointing. I saw one of the pygmy's poisoned thorns. It was fixed in the wood where Holmes and I had been standing. The poisoned thorn had passed through the air between us.

Holmes was smiling, but I felt cold and sick. We had escaped a horrible death.

As we went back up the river, we shone our light on the water. We were looking for the body of the pygmy. But we saw nothing. His body still lies somewhere at the bottom of the River Thames.

14
The Treasure is Lost

The wooden-legged man was our prisoner. He was sitting in the police launch opposite the treasure chest.

He was about fifty years old. He had black, curly hair and a black beard. He did not look angry any more. He was not interested in anything.

'What's your name?' Holmes asked him.

'Jonathan Small,' replied the man.

'Jonathan Small,' repeated Holmes. He took out the piece of paper which had been found in Captain Morstan's luggage.

Holmes read out what was written on the piece of paper, '"Jonathan Small, Mahomet Singh, Abdullah Khan, Dost Akbar. The Sign of Four".'

'Give me that paper,' said the man. Holmes gave it to him.

'Yes,' Small said, 'I am one of The Sign of Four. This paper is a plan of the fortress[30] at Agra in India. My three friends and I found the treasure many years ago. Tonight I have lost the Agra Treasure and you have killed my dear friend, Tonga. I am not sorry about the deaths of Sholto and his son. I'm not sorry about anything. Do what you like with me.'

The Treasure is Lost

'You will tell us your story later,' said Holmes. 'But first, Watson, would you take the treasure to Miss Morstan?'

'I shall be pleased to do that,' I said.

But I was not speaking the truth. I did not want to take the treasure to Miss Morstan. I did not want her to become a rich woman.

'Inspector Jones and I will take our prisoner to Baker Street,' said Holmes. 'We'll meet you there, Watson.' Then Holmes turned to Jonathan Small. 'But where is the key of the treasure chest?'

'At the bottom of the river,' replied Jonathan Small.

'Why did you throw it away?' cried Inspector Jones angrily. 'You have made things very difficult for us.'

Jonathan Small did not speak. He did not care what Jones said.

When we got to the jetty, I got out of the launch with the treasure chest. I found a cab and drove to Miss Morstan's house.

Miss Morstan was sitting by the window. She was wearing a pretty, white dress and her hair was shining brightly in the lamplight.

'How nice to see you,' she said when she saw me. 'Do you have any news?'

'I have brought something better than news,' I said, trying to speak happily. 'I have brought the Agra Treasure.'

I put the heavy chest down on the table. Miss Morstan did not look very excited.

'So, this is the famous Agra Treasure,' she said.

'Yes,' I replied. 'Half of it belongs to you and half to Thaddeus Sholto. You are a rich woman now, Miss Morstan.'

'The treasure can wait,' she said. 'First, I want to hear all about your adventures. Please sit down and tell me everything.'

So I told her everything that had happened. I told her how Holmes found the *Aurora*. I told her about Inspector Jones and Thaddeus Sholto. I told her about the chase on the river, the death of the pygmy and how we had caught Jonathan Small.

The Treasure is Lost

'How brave you are,' she said. 'I didn't know that you were in such terrible danger.'

'It's finished now,' I said. 'Let's open the treasure chest. There isn't a key. How can we open the chest?'

Miss Morstan left the room and came back with a heavy metal bar. I took the bar and put it under the lid of the chest.

Then I turned it and the lid opened. It lifted up the lid. My hands were shaking. We both looked inside. Then we looked at each other in astonishment. The chest was empty! The chest was made of very thick iron. This was why it was so heavy.

'The treasure is lost,' said Miss Morstan quietly.

'Thank God!' I said.

'Why do you say "Thank God"?' asked Miss Morstan.

'Because now I can ask you to marry me,' I replied, holding her hand. 'Because I love you, Mary. Now you are not going to be rich.

So I can tell you my feelings. That is why I said "Thank God".'
'Then I say "Thank God" too,' she whispered.

15
The Sign of Four

When I got back to Baker Street, Holmes, Inspector Jones and the prisoner, Jonathan Small, were all waiting for me. I showed them the empty treasure chest. Small began to laugh.

'Where is the treasure, Small?' shouted Jones angrily.

'The Agra Treasure belongs to the Sign of Four,' said Small quietly. 'No one else will have it. I threw it all to the bottom of the river.'

We all stood astonished. The great treasure of Agra was lost for ever.

'The Agra Treasure is unlucky,' said Small. 'It has never brought happiness to anyone. It brought death to Captain Morstan. It brought fear and guilt to Major Sholto. Bartholomew Sholto was murdered because of it. And to me and the other members of the Sign of Four, it has brought prison for the rest of our lives.'

'You must tell us your story,' said Holmes. 'What is the Sign of Four?'

Jonathan Small began his strange story and we listened.

'I went to India as a soldier in the British Army,' said Small. 'One day, soon after I arrived, I had an accident and lost my leg. After that, I could not fight any more.

'Then there was terrible fighting between the Indians and the British. The British all hid in an old fortress at Agra. They shut themselves inside. The walls of this fortress were very thick. The Indians could not get in.

The Sign of Four

'I also went to Agra. I had three Indian friends who had fought for the British. They came to Agra with me These men were Mahomet Singh, Abdullah Khan and Dost Akbar. When we were in the Agra fortress, we heard a strange story. It was about a great treasure which had been hidden in the fortress. It had been hidden for many years. The four of us decided to look for this treasure. And one day we found it. It was hidden under the floor in a secret room.

'We were astonished by what we had found. We had never seen so many beautiful jewels. The four of us decided not to say anything about what we had found. We decided to leave the treasure hidden in the secret room in the fortress. When the fighting was finished, we would be able to take the treasure away with us.

'We made a promise to each other. We agreed that we would always work together. We would share the treasure between us.

We became the Sign of Four. But a terrible thing happened. Two British soldiers were killed in a fight. We had not killed them but we were arrested for their murder. We were sent to prison in the Andaman Islands.'

'Is that where you met Major Sholto and Captain Morstan?' asked Holmes.

'Yes,' said Small. 'Sholto and Morstan were the officers in charge of the prisoners there.

'We were in a terrible situation. We knew where the Agra Treasure was. But we were not able to go and get it. We were prisoners. Also, we were afraid that someone else might find the treasure. We did not know what to do. At last we told Sholto and Morstan about the great treasure. We asked them to help the four of us to escape. When we were free, we would get the treasure and share it with them. But Sholto said that he did not believe us. He said he did not know if we were speaking the truth. Sholto did not know if the treasure would be there. He said he would go to India. If he found the treasure, he would come back. He would help us escape from prison. Sholto asked the four of us to give him a plan of the fortress at Agra.

'We did not want to give Sholto the plan. I didn't trust him. But in the end we had to agree. We gave one plan to Sholto and another to Morstan. Sholto went to India. But he never came back. He found the treasure and took it to England. He stole it from the Sign of Four and also from his friend Morstan. And from that day, I decided to have revenge on Sholto.'

Small was silent for a few moments. He was thinking about what Sholto had done. Then he went on with his story.

'I made friends with one of the people of the Andaman Islands,' he said. 'The people there are pygmies. They are very small, but they are very brave.

'One day, I found one of these pygmies lying under a tree. He was very ill. I looked after him. He slowly got better. He became my friend. His name was Tonga.

'Tonga helped me to escape from the islands. He had a small boat. One dark night, we put lots of food into the boat and we sailed together from the Andaman Islands.'

Holmes had been listening carefully while Small told his story. Now he spoke, 'Ah - I understand,' he said, 'Major Sholto received a letter. What was written in the letter frightened him to death. It must have been the news of your escape which killed him.'

Small went on with his story. 'At last Tonga and I reached London. But I was too late to have revenge on Sholto. Sholto was dying. He saw my face at the window. That night I got into his room and left a message. It was from The Sign of Four.

'Tonga and I waited six years. We watched Pondicherry Lodge and Bartholomew Sholto carefully. When Bartholomew Sholto found the treasure, we knew about it immediately. With Tonga's help, I got into his room. Tonga killed Bartholomew Sholto with a poisoned thorn. We took the treasure, left the paper and went.

'I had paid Mordecai Smith to take us to a ship. We were planning to go to America. But now everything has changed. Tonga is dead and I am your prisoner. And the Agra Treasure is lost for ever.'

We were all silent. We were thinking of the great treasure which was lost in the mud at the bottom of the River Thames. Perhaps it was better there.

'Doctor Watson,' said Holmes, when Inspector Jones had taken Small away, 'that is the end of our adventure.'

'Yes,' I said. 'But I have some very good news. Miss Morstan and I are going to get married.'

'Excellent,' said Holmes. 'The Agra Treasure has at last brought happiness to someone.'

Points for Understanding

1

1 Why did Doctor Watson return to England?
2 How did Sherlock Holmes help his clients?
3 Why was Holmes bored?
4 Who was Holmes' new client?

2

1 Miss Morstan went to a hotel in London and asked for her father. What did the hotel manager tell her?
2 What was Captain Morstan's job in India?
3 Who was Major Sholto?
4 The next day Miss Morstan received a small cardboard box.
   (a) What was in the box?
   (b) How many times did she receive the same sort of box?
5 Miss Morstan had come to see Sherlock Holmes because she had received a note.
   (a) Where was she to go that night at seven o'clock?
   (b) Who could she bring with her?
   (c) How was the note signed?
6 What did Holmes decide to do?

3

1 Why did Holmes think that Major Sholto's death was important?
2 Miss Morstan showed Holmes a piece of paper.
   (a) Where had she found it?
   (b) What was drawn on the paper?
   (c) How was the paper signed?
3 Who did Holmes, Watson and Miss Morstan meet at the Lyceum Theatre?
4 Where did they go?

4

1. Why was Doctor Watson angry with Thaddeus Sholto?
2. Thaddeus Sholto and his brother, Bartholomew, knew that their father was afraid of something. Who did their father think was following him?
3. Why did their father become very ill?
4. When Captain Morstan and Major Sholto were in India they found a great treasure.
   (a) What was the name of this treasure?
   (b) Why did Captain Morstan and Major Sholto argue?
   (c) How did the argument end?
5. What did Major Sholto ask his sons to do?
6. Thaddeus and his brother, Bartholomew found a note on the bed beside their father's body. What words were written on the note?

5

1. Why did Thaddeus Sholto send the letter to Miss Morstan?
2. Where was the treasure?
3. Why was Doctor Watson unhappy?
4. Where did Thaddeus Sholto take Miss Morstan, Holmes and Watson?
5. Where had Bartholomew Sholto found the treasure chest?
6. When they arrived at Pondicherry Lodge, the house was dark.
   (a) What noise did they hear?
   (b) Who opened the door?
   (c) What did she say to Thaddeus Sholto?

6

1. What did Holmes and Watson see through the keyhole?
2. How did Bartholomew Sholto die?
3. What else made Thaddeus Sholto upset?

7

1. How did Holmes know that a man with a wooden leg had been in the room?
2. How did Watson think the wooden-legged man had got into the room?
3. What was strange about the footprints in the thick dust?
4. Describe murderer Number One.

8

1 Why did the murderers kill Major Sholto and Bartholomew Sholto?
2 Why was Holmes pleased that one of the murderers had stepped in the creosote?
3 Why did Inspector Jones not want to listen to Sherlock Holmes?
4 Who did Inspector Jones think the murderer was?

9

1 What two things did Holmes ask Watson to do?
2 What was special about the dog, Toby?
3 How did the pygmy get up onto the roof of the Pondicherry Lodge?
4 'He's on the trail!' cried Holmes. What trail had Toby found?

10

1 Why was Toby not able to follow the trail when they got to the River Thames?
2 Where had Mordecai Smith gone?
3 Who had gone with him?
4 Why was Mrs Smith worried?

11

1 Why did Holmes not want to contact the police?
2 What did Holmes show Watson in the newspaper?
3 Why did the ragged children make such good agents for Holmes?

12

1 Doctor Watson went to tell Miss Morstan that they had not found the treasure. That night he could not sleep. What was Watson thinking about?
2 How had Inspector Jones changed?
3 Where was the *Aurora* hidden?
4 What were the murderers planning to do?

13

1 Suddenly a launch came out of the boatyard. How did they know that it was the *Aurora*?
2 'We fired our guns together.' Why did Holmes and Watson shoot at the pygmy?
3 What happened to the pygmy?
4 Why was the wooden-legged man not able to escape?
5 What did Holmes and Watson think was in the big, heavy chest?
6 How had Holmes and Watson escaped a horrible death?

14

1 Who was Jonathan Small?
2 Why did Watson not want to take the treasure to Miss Morstan?
3 Why was Watson much happier after the chest had been opened?

15

1 What had happened to the Great Agra Treasure?
2 Who were the Sign of Four? Where did they meet?
3 How did Jonathan Small meet Captain Morstan and Major Sholto?
4 Holmes said, 'The Great Agra Treasure has at last brought happiness to someone.' To whom had it brought happiness?

Glossary

1. **private detective** (page 4)
   someone who finds out how a crime happened and then tries to find the criminal. Sherlock Holmes is not a policeman, he is a private detective. But sometimes he helps the police solve crimes or find criminals.
2. **client** (page 4)
   someone who comes to Sherlock Holmes and asks for help.
3. **impatiently** (page 5)
   Holmes is bored. He wants something exciting to happen.
4. **housekeeper** (page 5)
   a woman who looks after a house and the people living in it.
5. **tray** (page 5)
   the people in this story lived in the nineteenth century. When a visitor arrived at someone's house he or she gave the servant a card. The visitor's name and address was on the card. The servant then put the card on a tray and took it to the owner of the house. In this story, the housekeeper brings the card to Sherlock Holmes on a silver tray.
6. **advertised** (page 7)
   the police printed special messages in newspapers. These messages asked Captain Morstan to come to them.
7. **ornaments** (page 7)
   ornaments are small objects which are put in a room to make it beautiful. Captain Morstan had collected many beautiful things on his travels in the world.
8. **old copies of the newspaper** (page 10)
   newspaper offices usually keep one copy of every newspaper they have printed. People can find out what happened in the past by looking at these old copies.
9. **cab** (page 11)
   a carriage pulled by a horse. There were no motor vehicles at the time of this story.
10. **magnifying glass** (page 11)
    a glass you look through that makes things seem larger.

11 *astonished* (page 14)
very surprised.
12 *share* (page 17)
Morstan is asking for the part of the treasure he thinks he should have.
13 *guilt* (page 17)
a feeling of fear and worry because you have done something wrong.
14 **treasure chest** (page 20)
a large, strong box containing valuable jewels and gold.
15 *thorn* (page 23)
a sharp point that grows on the branches of some trees and bushes.
16 *poisoned* (page 23)
poison is something which can kill a person if it gets into their body. Poison has been put on the sharp end of the thorn. If the thorn cuts someone, the poison will get into their blood and kill them.
17 *windowsill* (page 25)
a flat shelf at the bottom of a window.
18 **set of steps** (page 26)
wooden stairs that can be carried from one place to another. See illustration on page 24.
19 *dwarf* (page 27)
a person who is unusually small in height.
20 *pygmy* (page 28)
pygmies are a group of people who are unusually small. Pygmies live in parts of Africa and Asia.
21 *revenge* (page 28)
the Sign of Four have agreed that they will find and kill the Sholto family because the family stole the treasure.
22 **creosote** (page 29)
a dark brown liquid with a very strong smell. Creosote is used to protect wood.
23 **arrest** – *I arrest you . . .* (page 31)
the words used by police officers when they catch criminals.
24 **lead** (page 34)
a long, thin piece of leather. A lead is fixed to a collar on the neck of a dog to stop it running away.
25 *drainpipe* (page 34)
a long pipe on the side of a house. Drainpipes carry the water off the roof of the house when it rains.

26 *jetty* (page 37)
    a strong wooden platform built from the land into the water. People step from the jetty into boats.
27 **steam launch for hire** (page 37)
    a steam launch is a boat whose engine is driven by steam. Steam comes from water heated by burning coal. People pay Mordecai Smith to use his boats and steam launch.
28 **funnel** (page 40)
    the smoke from the burning coal on a steam launch comes out through the funnel. See illustration on page 47.
29 **boatyard** (page 45)
    a large building where boats are built or repaired.
30 **fortress** (page 49)
    a strong building used by soldiers during wars.

Exercises

True or False?

Write T (True) or F (False).

1. | F | Sherlock Holmes was a policeman.
2. | | Sherlock Holmes was a private detective.
3. | | Sherlock Holmes lived at 221B Baker Street, London.
4. | | Dr Watson was a police inspector.
5. | | Sherlock Holmes never had anything to do with the police.

Unanswered Questions

a) After talking to Miss Morstan, Holmes made some notes. How many questions could he answer before he met Thaddeus Sholto? Complete the gaps.

	QUESTION	ANSWER
1	When did Captain Morstan disappear?	
2	Where did Captain Morstan live and work?	
3	Is Captain Morstan dead?	
4	Did Captain Morstan have a friend in London?	
5	Has Mary tried to find this friend?	
6	Who sends a pearl to Mary every year?	
7	What paper was in Captain Morstan's luggage?	

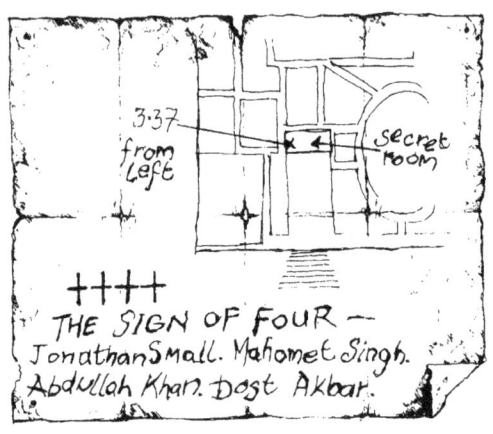

8	How many names are on the paper?	
9	Are they English names?	
10	Was something hidden in the secret room?	

b) Which questions could Holmes answer by the end of the story? Complete the gaps.

QUESTION	ANSWER

Multiple Choice 1

Tick the best answer.

1 Who worked with Captain Morstan in the Andaman Islands?
a ☑ Major Sholto.
b ☐ Jonathan Small.

2 Who returned to London first?
a □ Major Sholto.
b □ Captain Morstan.

3 Where did Captain Morstan go as soon as he returned to London?
a □ To visit his daughter.
b □ To visit Major Sholto.

4 What information did Sherlock Holmes find from *The Times* newspaper?
a □ The date of death of Captain Morstan.
b □ The date of death of Major Sholto.

5 What connection did Holmes make between the date of death and the pearls?
a □ The pearls arrived around the anniversary of Captain Morstan's death.
b □ The pearls arrived around the anniversary of Major Sholto's death.

6 How did Thaddeus Sholto explain Captain Morstan's disappearance?
a □ He said he went to Agra in India.
b □ He said he died in Major Sholto's house.

7 Why did Captain Morstan go to Major Sholto's house?
a □ To kill Major Sholto.
b □ To claim his share of the Agra Treasure.

8 Why did Thaddeus Sholto want Miss Morstan to go to Pondicherry Lodge?
a □ To claim her share of the Agra Treasure.
b □ To meet his brother.

The Death of Bartholomew Sholto

Complete the gaps. Use each word in the box once.

> died   murder   been   hours   stiff   ear   killed   picked
> thorn   treasure   showed   read   pain   could   sticking
> face   poisoned   piece   dead   table

Bartholomew Sholto was [1] *dead*. He was sitting in a chair by a [2]............... . His body was [3]............... and cold. I [4]............... see that he had [5]............... dead for many [6]............... . The dead man's body was twisted with [7]............... . There was a horrible smile on his [8]............... .

There was a [9]............... of paper on the body. Holmes [10]............... it up and read it.

He [11]............... it to me. In the light of the lamp, I [12]............... with horror - The Sign of Four. 'What does it mean?' I asked.

'It means [13]...............,' Holmes replied. He pointed to Bartholomew Sholto's [14]............... . 'Look.'
I looked. I saw something [15]............... in the dead man's skin near his ear.

'It looks like a [16]...............,' I said.

'It is a thorn,' said Holmes. 'You can take it out, but be careful. It is [17]............... .'

'So this is how Bartholomew Sholto [18]...............,' I said. 'What a terrible death. But who [19]............... him? And why?'

We had forgotten about Thaddeus Sholto. He was still standing in the doorway. Suddenly he gave a cry. 'The [20]............... has gone!' he cried. 'They have stolen the treasure.'

Multiple Choice 2

Tick the best answer.

1 How did Holmes and Watson get into the room where Bartholomew Sholto had been murdered?
a ☐ Thaddeus Sholto let them in.
b ☐ The housekeeper opened the door.
c ☐ They broke the door down.
d ☐ They climbed through the window.

2 How did murderer 'Number One' get into the room?
a ☐ He had a key.
b ☐ He climbed through the hole in the ceiling.
c ☐ He came down the chimney.
d ☐ He came up through the floor.

3 What strange marks did Holmes see on the floor of the secret room?
a ☐ The number 4 written in blood.
b ☐ The footprints of a dog.
c ☐ The imprint of large boots.
d ☐ Some very small footprints.

4 What did Holmes conclude from these marks?
a ☐ That one of the murderers was a pygmy.
b ☐ That one murderer had big feet.
c ☐ That a child had climbed into the room.
d ☐ That the murderer had used a monkey.

5 What was the strong smell in the room?
a ☐ Blood.
b ☐ Perfume.
c ☐ Paint.
d ☐ Creosote.

6 How was Holmes able to follow the murderers?
a ☐ As soon as it was daylight he saw the marks of a wooden leg.
b ☐ The murderers had dropped jewels in the mud.
c ☐ He borrowed a dog which followed the smell of creosote to the river.
d ☐ The treasure chest had left marks in the ground.

Making Sentences

Write questions for the answers.

1 *What did Mordecai Smith hire?*
   Mordecai Smith hired boats and a steam launch.

2 What ....
   ....
   The name of the steam launch was the *Aurora*.

3 Who ....
   ....
   Mordecai Smith took the wooden-legged man with him in the *Aurora*.

4 Did ....
   ....
   No, Holmes did not tell the police that he was looking for the *Aurora*.

5 Who ....
   Holmes' agents on the river were children.

6 What ....
   Holmes wanted the agents to find the *Aurora*.

7 What ....
   Holmes gave his agents some money.

8 Who ....
   Holmes sent a telegram to Inspector Jones.

9 *Where*
....
   Holmes found the *Aurora* in a boatyard near the river.

10 *How*
....
....
   Holmes, Watson and Inspector Jones caught the murderers by chasing their boat along the river.

What Happened Next?

Number the sentences in the correct order to give the outline of the story.

☐ Small and the other three men were arrested and sent to prison in the Andaman Islands.

☐ They sent a message to Mary Morstan. They asked her to go to the Lyceum Theatre.

☐ Small told Morstan and Sholto where the treasure was hidden.

☐ After six years, the brothers found the treasure in the roof of their father's house.

☐ Morstan went to London to find Sholto.

[1] Jonathan Small and three Indian friends found a chest of treasure in Agra.

☐ Jonathan Small escaped from prison with the help of a pygmy called Tonga.

☐ Jonathan Small and Tonga broke into the Sholtos' house and killed Bartholomew.

☐ Sholto hid Morstan's body and the Agra treasure.

☐ Morstan and Sholto had an argument and Morstan died of a heart attack.

☐ Sholto took the treasure to London and cheated the others.

☐ Before Major Sholto died, he told his sons Bartholomew and Thaddeus about the hidden treasure.

Words From the Story

Complete the gaps. Use each word in the box once.

> revenge   clients   advertised   astonished   guilt
> poisoned   arrest   pygmy   share

1 Mary Morstan was ......*astonished*...... when she received a pearl through the post.
2 She .... her address in the newspaper when she read that someone was looking for her.
3 Sherlock Holmes liked to have interesting .... to work for.
4 Jonathan Small wanted to take his .... on Major Sholto because he had deceived him.
5 Small made friends with a .... from the Andaman Islands.
6 Tonga killed Bartholomew Sholto with a .... thorn.
7 Morstan went to see Major Sholto to ask him for his .... of the Agra Treasure.
8 Holmes did not want Inspector Jones to .... Thaddeus Sholto.
9 Major Sholto told his sons that he felt great .... because he had kept the Agra Treasure all for himself.

Multiple Choice 3

Tick the best answer.

1 How did Thaddeus and Bartholomew find Miss Morstan?
a ☐ They hired a private detective.
b ☐ They looked in the telephone directory.

c ☐ They advertised in the newspaper.
d ☐ They guessed she lived in her father's old house.

2 How did Thaddeus and Bartholomew find the treasure?
a ☐ They dug up the garden.
b ☐ They looked under all the floor boards in the house.
c ☐ They found the key to a secret room.
d ☐ They compared the outside and inside measurements of the house.

3 When did Miss Morstan find out that her father was dead?
a ☐ When Thaddeus Sholto told her.
b ☐ Three days after he disappeared.
c ☐ Four years after he disappeared.
d ☐ When she received the sixth pearl.

4 Why did Small leave the message THE SIGN OF FOUR on Bartholomew's body?
a ☐ It was the name of the four men who had been cheated of the treasure.
b ☐ It was the name of the poison used by Tonga to kill him.
c ☐ He wanted to kill four people.
d ☐ It was the name of the place where he could be found.

5 Who shared the Agra Treasure in the end?
a ☐ Miss Morstan and Thaddeus Sholto.
b ☐ Tonga and Jonathan Small.
c ☐ Sherlock Holmes and Dr Watson.
d ☐ No one because it was lost in the river.

6 For whom did the story end most happily?
a ☐ For Thaddeus Sholto.
b ☐ For Jonathan Small.
c ☐ For Mordecai Smith.
d ☐ For Dr Watson and Mary Morstan.

Macmillan Education Limited
4 Crinan Street
London N1 9XW

Companies and representatives throughout the world

Macmillan Readers Intermediate Sign of Four, The
ISBN: 978-1-035-15100-4
Macmillan Readers Intermediate Sign of Four, The with eBook and Resources
ISBN: 978-1-035-15103-5

This is a retold version by Anne Collins of the original work by Sir Arthur Conan Doyle.
Text © Anne Collins 1983, 1992, 1998, 2002, 2005, 2024
Design and illustration © Macmillan Education Limited 1998, 2002, 2005, 2024

First published 1983
This edition published 2024

All rights reserved. No part of this publication may be reproduced, stored in a retrieval system, or transmitted in any form or by any means, electronic, mechanical, photocopying, recording, or otherwise, without the prior written permission of the publishers.

Illustrated by Kay Dixie
Cover photograph by Getty/Huizeng Hu

Printed and bound in
2028   2027   2026   2025   2024
10 9 8 7 6 5 4 3 2 1